Max Wickert

ALL THE WEIGHT
OF THE STILL MIDNIGHT

Second, Expanded Edition

Outriders Poetry Project
Buffalo, NY 2013

ISBN-13: 978-0-9841772-6-4
ISBN-10: 0-9841772-6-4

A first, much shorter edition of this work was published in 1972 as an Outriders chapbook and consisted of selections from three sequences: "Departures," "Nocturnes" and "Serenades". This second edition restores the poems omitted from the chapbook and adds the previously unpublished "Elegy".

The following first appeared in journals and anthologies as noted:

Departures nos. 1, 3 and 5 in *Presence*; nos. 2, 7, 10, 14 and 25 in *Michigan Quarterly Review*; no. 2 in Philip Dacey and John Knoll (ed.), *I Love You All Day It Is That Simple* (St. Meinrad, Indiana: Abbey Press, 1970); no. 7 in Dennis Maloney (ed.), *On Turtle's Back* (Buffalo, New York: White Pine Press, 1979); nos. 4 & 18 in *Buffalo Courier Express Sunday Magazine*; nos. 8, 15 and 22 in *Prologue*; no. 16 in *Descant*; nos. 20 and 26 in *Choice* (Chicago).

Nocturnes: no. 7 in *The Reporter* (Buffalo); nos. 8 and 13 in *Poetry* (Chicago).

Serenades: no. 7 in *The Buffalo News Poetry Page*.

Cover photo: Richard Puell

In Memoriam
Joanne Martiny Conroy
Ann London Scott
Shreela Ray
Elaine Schwartz
&
Monika Andrews

TABLE OF CONTENTS

ALL THE WEIGHT
OF THE STILL MIDNIGHT

DEPARTURES

1 When the bell has rung, the inward world
    will be torn away. The sudden child
    will leap from his mother's agony
    and in the twinkling of an eye
    husband and wife will turn from the lie
    of marriage.
                As soon as the bell sounds
    will be the time of departures. Words
    will hurry out of the useless brain
    and the fire of the earth will burn
    to rush away from its flesh of stone.

    The bell will hardly have rung when blood
    will run from blood and when all the gold
    in the earth will be suddenly spent.
    Quickly the bright body will depart
    from the jail of soul. Quicker than that,
    too quickly, the poet abandons
    his poem.
                Now the bell rings. He runs.

2 THE MONTHS

There is so little left of my now —
a few feathers stuck to a shovel,
my stink lingering in the gravel,
the final cadence of my slow cry
garbled in a rushing of water.

You there, on your chair in the parlor,
combing your hair and full of tears, you
are also full of my life. You grow
big-bellied as I fade into air.
What a long wait it is to silence,

what weary flight to complete absence.
Your hair is crackling beneath your comb
as you feel my first kick in your womb.
My shadow behind the window panes
moves a little further out of sight.

In the fourth month, I return at night
rustling wings in my dream of farewells,
a black beak worrying your nipples.
In the early dawn, you sit up straight
and hear soft wailing from the kitchen.

I am between your heart and the sun,
forever saying goodbye, never
going away. Life is half over.
It comes and goes at once. You begin
to feel your backbone aching with me.

Your footfall on the stairs is heavy.
Who could predict that it takes so long?
I know I should stop hesitating
behind your threshold and fly away.
You've already forgotten my name.

In a little while, I will become
indistinguishable from the rain-
drops' tattoo upon your window pane
or from the low unremitting drum
of your pulse. And now the rain must end.

O my girl, I have brought you to bed,
chained you to the rack of my parting.
Soon I will make you scream for my long
fall out of knowledge into the red
heat of your blood. I am finished. See,

there is nothing at all left of me.
My soiled life drops out of you, and soon
the rough tongue of time will lick me clean.
You smile and I cry my infant cry.
You will not remember me. Goodbye.

3 Goodnight, goodnight, and now go to sleep.
  We've talked too much and it's hard to stop.
  Sometimes I think you're all in my head,
  that you spill from my mouth with each word,
  rise to my brain with my blood, grow ripe
  in the tears I don't shed. When the lamp

  is out though —when you doze off and sprawl
  solidly against my back, I feel
  I have no such stakes in you. I see
  it is your presence leaves me empty,
  fidgeting for property, a fool
  with dreams about a farmyard idyll.

  It's not that you rule in my mind, no,
  nor body. It's that you're there below
  my pressure, under my eyes, always,
  even through nights in which I'm dreamless.
  What do I have for myself?
  Who really fills my soul? If only you

  weren't here, I could tell what I own:
  Up there are my two vineyards. All mine.
  This is my plow field. My well. My grass.
  This is my barn full of wheat. This is
  my very own mossy dark ravine.
  And over here is a long way down.

4 The outward world is taken away.
   I can't listen any longer, I
   can't look at you. But I see a bright
   danger as I close my eyes. A great
   hum as of gongs is shaking like rain
   through the silence at my ears. Our son
   smiles an angry smile somewhere among
   tangles of unbearable lightning;
   his laughter frightens me because it
   echoes everywhere, nowhere. His foot
   kicks at all gates and his fingers pull
   at a thousand window slats. He will
   get to me before he gets to you, pin
   me down in a world not my own.
   And he'll pretend to be right at home.
   Then it will be your turn. The small flame
   at which you stare each night will grow pale
   and tremble while you shiver to feel
   your house belong to another. See,
   darling, I'm gone. When finally
   the inward world is taken away
   I will look to your small light and I
   will listen for your terrible cry.

5 The foolish husband bound to his house
    complains. He's difficult to locate.
    Find out the wife first. It's her story
    will make his mumbling clear. The nonsense
    of marriage now. The dumb cowardice.

    A married woman should have no past.
    She should take a man who is virgin.
    They should suddenly leave the city,
    dance like wildfires in the desert waste,
    visible, exposed, courageous, lost.

    This is what should be. But then the facts
     are otherwise. The bride at the church
    whores after her girl-hood. Her body
    tingles with the scars of years, contracts
    and throbs with ancient twitches and aches.

    She is stiff with white veils. The bridegroom
    mopes after her from room to room. Lost
    to themselves they trade for a baby.
    Husband, what are you? Your house is a dream.
    Go away. Your wife is not at home.

6 Over here I walk with freer breath.
   Taking things as they are, leaving things
   as they are, 'I have forgotten youth.
   The face of my sister coarsening
   in marriage smiles kindly from the bark
   of every tree that grows. My father
   hides in the tall grass, a mossy rock
   I rest on. My still unborn brother
   sings from a black cricket hole. And I
   see but I do not look, I hear but
   do not listen.
                    Even while you die,
   mother, your eyes too shine in the lights
   of the fireflies and your hard palms
   keep the woodpecker's nest. The small bones
   of your aching feet roll in clear streams.
   Your name is marked on all trees and stones
   and I walk more slowly here until
   your dying makes me stand wholly still.

7 There is no answer to your question
and if you know this already, then

you shouldn't ask. I'm not what you think
I am. I have no wealth and must break

the links of your clenched hand, overcome
your need to spare your language. I am

the fine selfishness lying in wait
behind your teeth, the other heartbeat

sucking at the shy surge of your blood.
I am the pressure behind your child.

I'll be leaving now. Not you, but I
make the demands here. So don't ask why.

If I married you for your money
you have to be rich. Thank you; thank you.

8 All right then, I will tell you again
   and for once please listen. My reason
   for praising you is I take pleasure
   in your body chiefly from afar.

   And don't stare at nothing, look at me,
   remember you started this. I say
   you are lovely because I have sent
   you postcards. Can you understand that?

   Pay attention. Can you? And I spoke
   of your beauty because I mistook
    it for something else when I was drunk,
   something weak or defenseless I think.

   Why so distracted? If you don't want
   to hear this why did you ask? You bent
   over me once and I knew your face
   was too dark for me to embarrass

   with flattering. But since that one time
   it was no flattery to become
   the vocal fool of your faraway,
   luminous, threatened outline, betray

   yourself to yourself in a letter.
   Oh, all right, it might have been better
   to say nothing. But you would not hear
   how even the silences change gear.

   Listen now, I am telling you that
   you are beautiful. But huge secret
   wheels rumble in the hangover earth.
   Listen. I praise you with your own breath.

9 I said what I had to say. I know
   you have feelings too. Wasn't it you
   who taught me once to hear the clock tick.

   But it all mounts up. The drops collect
   in the rain barrel and the mornings
   grow quieter and much colder. Things
   clutter up the untraveled back roads
   and the noise the children make recedes
   mile after mile.
                    I've grown used to it.
   Day by day more and more I forgot
   the small groups of gesticulating
   people out of earshot, the hurt young girl
   waving from across the river,
   the rumors of small towns on fire.

   I had savage silence, it was all
   I had. The hours were beautiful
   and I said so. I am not sorry
   and treasure these things in my mind.
                                    Please
   come and put them away. Lay your hand
   across my eyes. Let me look at blood.

10 The pitch black comes and I am in it
    riding toward your vanishing house.
    Make ready for the sable planet.

    It melts the horizon in its rise
    and I am in it. I am coming
    into the far corners of your eyes.

    Faster than you think the glistening
    lake surface turns to steel and the steel
    dissolves in my solid air. The long

    highways vanish. Every animal
    bursts its skin and the sap of blossoms
    boils up pell-mell with rocks. What you smell

    are hints of my hot metal. It comes
    quickly and it is quickly over.
    And I make haste in those lightless beams.

    They come. I love you. Stay indoors,
    bolt them out, don't let them shine on you.

    What you almost hear is my sorrow.

II One night last summer when you were gone
    I took your necklace and spread it on
    my chest and felt how heavy and cool
    it was. Today's minutes leave a chill
    like those pearls on the string on my skin.
    I shouldn't enjoy being alone.

    Lady of pearls, you cook my red soup.
    Friends drop from my hands and feet.
    I grope for myself when I go home from school.
    (Away from home I'm sentimental.)
    The cool minutes lie over my words
    like rows upon rows of heavy pearls.

    Someone talks to me who is not you,
    who does not have a friend's voice but grew
    in the minutes of my solitude.
    I see a body sexual and round.,
    my heavy hermaphrodite of love,
    talking as he leans over his stove.

    Your necklace hangs around his black throat.
    I eat his supper with my friends. But
    I remember it was you who said:
    Talk to me! Talk to me! Something red
    streaks down the blackness before my eyes.
    I dream constantly of long journeys.

12 And why should I destroy the language
   when cold flesh goes elsewhere anyhow?

   Crooked shadows on the sun-warped snow
   are redeeming vertical buildings.

   Or is it brightness that devours
   the stubborn stones with its dazzling teeth?

   Why aren't you here? I have come from
   another country and long for you.

   At least be here in the, next snowfall
   or in the next night without a moon.

   I will say this again and again
   when shadows slip away in darkness

   and high houses appear to dissolve
   in the black moonless snow. What are you

   waiting for? Must towers all fall down
   or language grow wholly adequate?

   Having come from another country
   I think this language is good enough.

13 I pass on: the rocks close behind me,
    the patterns of their veins fade out,
    caverns fill with sediment. You flee,
    already contracted to a point
    on the horizon where all lines meet.

    My nervous hands fumble over stone:
    Open, open up, let me in. Rocks
    close around me, I forget my skin.
    Things are turning inside out, the axe
    of my panic heart can't cut, it sticks.

    I have no choice but stand: Let me out.
    A stabbing pain at my side. Heavy
    pebbles roll rattling into my chest,
    I am filled with the cumbrous world,
    I lift my round eyes with difficulty.

    And there you are, finally, once again:
    Together we walk in the avenues
    of the inanimate earth. We learn
    it is stone, nothing but stone that says,
    Behold! I will be with you always.

14 My body is dispersed every night
slowly sinking in the loam of sleep.
My joints loosen, my skull opens up,
fingers and toes go groping about

by themselves, and I'm not astonished
if my quick eyes start out of my head.
Disordering myself in the mud
I create all that I ever wished.

Though I can't see the luminous shape
that I form all around me, I know
the foretaste of his milk and the slow
rocking ease of his procreant lap.

And I know who I am too when he
rises into the night from the ooze
and speaks his first word with my own voice.
 And what he says takes my breath away.

But when that word is spoken, my sleep
breaks and the shroud of my former skin
folds suddenly around me again.
I fall into waking as a trap

shuts over my partial self. And then
my eyes roll back like boulders to graves
and my mound of flesh is back in love
marked by my sex as by a tombstone.

Because I must assert this body
I hurl myself wildly on your clay.

15 No, leave me alone, I have nothing,
   nothing to say to you. Let me stand
   under the thick web of stars and pour
   out the warm liquid of my breath on

   the warm air. Let me feel the prickle
   of my pepper flesh rotting away.
   Don't come near me. No, my spittle
   is unpleasantly sweet and my brain

   a raisin shriveling with the moon.
   The filmy net in the sky lowers.,
   my fingertips reel it down around
   the black earth, around my heart. Never

   touch me, no, never look at my face —
   it fades, it is blurred in thickening meshes.
   Don't walk with me. No. my pace
   echoes away in the seething dew.

   I'm not at all what you think I am.
   No, not even the smear vanishing
   on the dawn is myself. Already
    it is a bad taste on the blue tongue

   of another day. No, do not ask
   what has become of me tomorrow.
   I've nothing to say to you. The last
   traces of my unsightly sorrow

   will be burned in the noonday sun.
   It is then your wounds will get better,
   your hate washed from your eyes.
   It is then you will see the night come and let her

   lead you to your pillow in the air.
   As for me: no, no I won't be there.

16 Under our very feet the earth turns.
   The loot of the fields fills up the barns.
   The moon is at all odds with itself:
   Love is not altogether enough.

   What next? This dancing makes me dizzy.
   Let's both get away from here and see
   the fields and forests spin while the stars
   suck at their holes in the sky. Who hears

   the hiss of escaping air? who feels
   the lascivious chill tug at the gills
   of the great fish of earth? —Anyway,
   all this play is nothing but foreplay.

   Above our heads it happens again:
   warfare of the man child with the crone.
   What can I say? You are much too old
   to go out with me into the cold.

17 My urge for girls in the flush of health
    brought me to you. I noticed your breath
    quicken as I rushed ashore to find
    that you were alone. You were afraid.

    I'm glad. How long I yearned for this!
    Take a last look now, feel the grass,
    watch the waves turn black, hear the lone magpie
    shriek, bend to the wilting blossoms. I
    heard of you; now I am here to see.

    I pause after I take off your clothes
    and am all unsatisfied. The grass
    is picking at the earth with its small knives.
    The thought drives me on, so I remove
    your skin and flesh. The bad weather
    of centuries cracks the rocks. So here
    I am chipping at your bones. And yet ,
    your marrow hides a fire to heat
    my zero chill. I can't fathom it.

    I have taken everything away
    from you. Still you are here. The magpie
    has fled with your eyes. Your threadbare dress
    and strands of your hair are drifting west
    on the sea. Still you are here. Flowers
    have eaten your heart. Still you are here.
    Your form flutters like the ghost of a flag
    in my wind. My snowdrifts melt and sag
    with your long-dry tears. Your lost hands dig

ever-changing patterns on my ice.
I've never been colder, and this
is not the place for me. Your terror
of meeting me endures forever.
If I could leave you as I found you
all things might be better. Anyhow,
it is time for me to travel west.
O love, love, see how I sally out —
a lewd shape in a rudderless boat.

18 Father, come on. It's time to get up.
   I'll nag you out of your bed of chaff.
   Wake up. Shake the earwigs from your ears,
   brush the dead leaves with clumsy fingers
   from your mammoth thigh. Come, be off:
   I can tell you this is no time for sleep.

   You've sprawled long enough gathering moss
   on your rough temples, your hair matted
   over the sly crocus, your knuckles
   rammed through the cracking ice. Now all hell's
   breaking loose, and I rise from the dead
   to raise you up. Listen to my voice.

   Listen for the droning, inside your skull,
   aching behind your blind eye; I pound
   the ruthless anvil under your ribs.
   The grass pushing at your back, the sobs
   of the fickle wind hiding behind
   bush and waterfall shout with my will.

   I know you won't like it, but the time
   is ripe. I must scourge you on once more,
   I, son of your loins, the small demon
   that loves and mocks you with the question,
   Father, father, where is my mother?
   I exult to see you rise and scream.

19 If afternoon comes, I want to lean
    against the weight of my shadow. When
    light grows crooked I want to fall down,
    my feet still on the same spot, my long
    shadow straining east as though to bring round
    my hands reaching west. A blinding
    last light must flash along the road that
    leads into the garden where you wait.

    If evening brings me even closer
    to you, the darkness must make you stir
    and your eyes open in a great stare
    should dissolve my every boundary.
    When nightmares loosen your tongue, then I
    should be drawn first by your cries, then by
    a sudden rain on my skin, and then
    by growls of thunder from your garden.

    But now bees crawl in the roadside dust.
    I won't lift this rock. The soil looks just
    as white below as above. To the west
    the horizon blurs with rising heat
    and the road melts away in a sheet
    of water to the east. Under it,
    I know, your invisible garden
    swims and hums in a remorseless noon.

    I stand stock still under the standing
    sun, for a step either way will bring
    me closer to your naked sweating
    body. My one way of leaving you
    is not to move at all. My shadow
    is wound up inside my skull for now.
    You wait in the garden. You are right.
    The sun won't always stand still like that.

20 Things happen when they're almost over.
    The tongue tastes a drink in the last drop.
    The final peach falls with the harvest.
    When nothing but the body is left
    we say: This is life.
                    But you and I
    gambled all our money on fresh starts,
    lived in houses and hoped they were home
    and called our children by name at birth.
    When first completely beside ourselves
    we said: We're in love.
                    I've made a map
    of your body because I wanted
    to understand where I had to go.
    I'm almost finished and will tell you
    tomorrow what your life is. But now
    show me the meaning of my last dream:

    My mother ran wailing, my father
    rotted in his coffin. I stood still
    as stone and muttered: This is only
    the beginning. After the moon rose
    I fondled her calloused hand and said:
    I'd rather go than send you away.
    Later my palm was groping for fruit
    in the bare branches of an orchard.
    Then I thought: Nothing can cure this thirst.
    The moon above me was almost full.

    This is the last picture in my brain.

21 And all will be well. The flakes of dust
    fall untouched from your lashes. You strain
    wrists, ankles to earth. The grass you brushed
    against has stained your belly green.

    My tongue has become a tongue of air
    to cut your blossom. Your bright rich skin
    has opened up without my pressure.
    Slowly my arms of rock drop you down.

    Turning your knees outward, you receive
    my ice, my storms twist between your breasts
    and my thumb points out your gold. The curve
    of your arched back grows tense. Your fruit bursts

    and the oils of all your aches flow, soak
    deep down into the soil. Your mouth tastes
    of salt, your eyes shine in the dark. Look!
    my thousand thoughts suck at small black teats.

    A secular bird, high in the air, soars,
    swoops, turns alone. His screams are silly.
    What has he lost? The morning nears.
    Dune grass stands up by the empty sea:

    a good time for going west, a wind
    for music on hollow bones. Goodbye.
    All will be well. I grow awake and
    find myself born on your green belly.

22 It's not me. What you fear is a word,
    a worm piercing to the buried girl,
    rotten wood giving way in a gloom
    full of small claws, the dark that moves
    its hooks of possibility, hoof-
    beats fading into the night, the pull
    of a dawn you think cruel.
                              Your bones,
    though, can hold you up and the cloak
    of your skin can fold you in a cloth
    stronger than you guess and no less soft.
    Your tall mortal body is a law
    to itself: all else is a thin fraud.
    My word steals the girl out of your loins
    to make more room for the growing boy.
    But I leave you to yourself, go out
    of your life and wish you well. So now
    you've nothing to fear.
                            The flower shuts
    in the night, the worm comes up, the sun
    ushers him to his tunneling. Calm,
    cold dawn is kinder than you thought. Ah!
    far away I see you wave goodbye —
    and do you smile now? You walk
    in light as no woman walks, no man,
    the fat grass at your feet rising in your tracks.

When you have gone I bask in the glare
of the morning and drowse off somewhere
into my new silence. I can smell
wormwood and fennel. Everything is wet
with daybreak. I hear cockcrows, the neigh
of a horse, my pulse like a great flail.
In the stillness you leave me my lips
move without words. An ache in my rib
and all my manhood goes away. Seed
spills out of me like a swarm of bees.

23 Shadows of fence-posts fall, the sun chews
        at the land's edge, an erotic chill
        comes up from the east.
                              Turn in disgust
        from the smell of earth, build a fire
        in the pot-bellied stove, relish reek
        of coal.
                    Outside, the enduring beasts
        awake, shoots and tendrils creak and snap,
        Spittlebugs bombard the roofing slats.

        The far city burns with a green light,
        a dull green light, it could hardly come
        from the houses, for the shades are down.
        Children long entombed would glow like that.

        Nature continues forever.
                              Wives
        in the dark plot the fall of their men.

        We've many things to be thankful for.

24 Your slim body in the rushes, in
    the wet places, gentle mistress of
    pale orange newts and whip-tail tadpoles
    and clear water —
                        I'll lie down with you
    on the bank of the creek and cherish
    your wet hair and skin, I'll shower you
    with small blue coins of forget-me-nots.

                    ✿

    This is my hole in the ground. "You know,
    your eyebrows look like faint smears of earth . . . "
    Leaf-mold rank in my nostrils, her I
    have given burial to the ghost-bird
    of my self esteem.
                        A naked tree
    gripping the soil so tightly.
                            A warning?

                    ✿

    Darling, winter fire, ice heat: eat
    these words, guilt-paper. Don't look at me.

                    ✿

    I'm silent about the air round us.
    In spring-time, in your other season,
    we breathe
            Love
                    into each other's mouths.

25 I love your fingers, the little bones
 in them, your shoulder blades when the light
 is on your back.
      And why aren't we
 frightened by the blaze in the west
 behind the buttonwoods? Sudden gold
 on our lips, and a queer voice somewhere,
 a wail of music from the rivers
 of Babylon.
     Stars.
       There will be fog—
 brook and flat valley milling with white
 dancers. Oh, the small bones. The sweetness.
    ✡

 A beast crashes through the dry thicket.
 Apples drop with a thud. Blades of grass
 snap, frost-brittle.
      Your lips at my mouth.

 I'm transparent, a giant of glass
 brooding on the edge of the dark world.
 Slowly the weight of the still midnight
 shifts onto my shoulders.
       The sweetness!
    ✡

 And Herod murdered all the children.
 Two toys lie broken on a white sheet.
 Two lovers awake.
      Thick smoke of blood
 rises to the sky. The animals
 are coming to the river to drink.
    ✡

 Love, you are all the morning I have.

. . . and again say goodbye, let it go
again, leave the skin, the house, the new
life in the scrappy old limbs. Cold, cold
blows the wind and breath is cold. The world
begs to be left alone. You and I
are through, again and again. Goodbye,
farewell, goodbye is our gospel, our
good news, our ultimate desire.
Amen, I will be with you always
cries the voice of the last stone, the voice
of the chill wind that blows upward-, up
through the tatters and holes of our sleep,
forsaking, releasing all we are
and all we will ever be elsewhere,
letting out the child in the belly,
the bee in the hollow tree, the cry
in the pain, the sweetness in the grape,
the red blood in the heart's covered cup,
the fire in the mountain, the brain
in the skull, the huge toad sleeping in
the stone of the world, the word
behind the teeth, the girl clutched in a boy's hand.

NOCTURNES

1 At moonrise they know it all
    behind the stars are brighter
    stars below the sleeping ground
    there lurks a deeper darkness
    after their cries of delight
    they mouth unutterable
    words and a cold rhythm throbs
    under their most excited
    heartbeats. In obscurity
    that leaps from their eyes the stars
    begin and in the fire
    that spreads from their foot-soles
    night stabs into the grave the words
    of the uncharted future
    are plotted out when they speak
    ultimate syllables time
    grows motoric as they breathe

    Moonrise and all is clear they
    converse in the most ancient
    of gestures grow silly fond
    with old anticipation
    of which something always comes
    though it is rarely their own
    doing and so they worry
    about the onset of dawn

    All would be well if morning
    taught them that their great yearning
    to grow up was also once
    an innocent desire

2 Absent-minded anyman
      anonymous on the moon
      can know neither here nor there
      it is all one to him now
      he has peeled his body bare
      and emptied out his whole mind
      has learned to keep his eye fixed
      on the milky way and his heart
      riveted to a single
      woman even if she is
      his mother.
                  All the same he
      knows "the perfume of flowers
      the beautification of
      the whole body night meetings
      in secret music token
      exchanges anguish remorse
      jealousy murder the whole
      opera"
                  though he perhaps
      can never be torn from his
      ivory chair and his play
      be nevermore entered
      or altered by spoil-sport dawn.

3 Open mouth of the moon and
   the youngest sons lie hidden
   pips inside a dark apple
   in the pulp of their sleeping
   from thousands of open mouths
   souls are protruding like mice

   Dull eyes of owls fall open
   wisdom spreads gigantic wings

   The green primitives prepare
   for the test of brotherhood
   now they're bidding goodbye
   to the heavy brutal voices
   of their first youth now scoring
   the soft face of the mother
   with delicate knives and now
   sweeping up moon dust into
   the deep hollow of a cheek

   They hurl their seed at the wall

   The mice dart in and out like
   tongues blades of wings cut the air
   clouds wipe the moon-mouth and peace
   composes trembling bowels
   whispers on thousands of lips

   Bedewed and calmed and strengthened
   once more the savages squeeze
   morning from the gourd of night

4 It is trial by moonlight:
   in this hot night human kind
   thrashes bravely on empty sheets
   no one will sleep with no one else
   muscles bulge arms flail
                         bravo!
   you keep your cushions at bay

   Memory my enemy
   goodnight: goodnight desire
   The loved one alone lies still
   how disappointing to find
   that the demons are friendly
   and her flesh only flowers

   But the disciple will dream
   a sentence pronounced over
   and over .
              On June 16th
   Nineteen-hundred-and-four you
   could still have endured your whole
   contemporaneity

   No one will be allowed in
   the Library.
                 Nowhere else
   morning comes down like an axe

5 Fly-by-night in boring talk
   the Sisters meet on cross-roads
   wait like stupid birds for our
   fires to die down in town
   Late the factories close late
   the disgruntled painter rips
   his canvas the countryside
   is sopped up by the road-maps

   Hello hello are those owls
   are there any owls left in
   this clinker-heap of a world?
   The last drunk on the street
   grins his fat mouth full of feathers

   Hello sky wet-nurse let's see
   those bosoms *One of these days*
   the pimp says *one of these days*
   I'll get married
                   Go to sleep!
   lights out in the fancy place!
   we hear everything (don't we)
   even faraway noises
   the talk of Sisters turning
   into the clicking of beaks

   Sirens wake us at dawn
                   Aiee!

6 Sober in their spotless night
   ghosts of lovers stand naked
   under every traffic light

   regard each other calmly
   and do not touch the dew falls
   down through them to the pavement

   the purposeless signals click
   Others lie leisurely side
   by side in the forsaken

   parking lots sit on the curb
   outside the Bank stroll *slowly*
   past the Armory every

   gesture and posture of theirs
   unhurried and decisive
   tender and reserved the dew

   drops through them the darkness
   includes their bright bodies these
   presences of the City

   and only you and I (love)
   know when their night is over
   and the hour when their cleanness

   passes, while new traffic
   trickles from the closed fist of
   the disenchanted morning

7 Because every blade of grass
points to a star and all light
has been lent to another
world,
        because wind and water
have enfranchised the swishing
of bare feet and the sleepy
cicadas,
        and because now
although the road is endless
the concrete of the road ends
at your toes,
          nobody knows
that a girl peels off her black
sweater in the pitch dark while
her man lies smiling and skinned
invisible even to
himself,
        and only the smell
tells field mice and foxes what
shape to give unfamiliar fright,
until night floats away
like a ghost in a garment
and morning paints nakedness
cleanly back on the landscape.

8   "Who whom"   boring old story
    of unhistorical owls
    while we two think to make it
    with you on top who whom
                           ho
    hum a fatuous question
    for such as exhaust themselves
    and have either like the owls
    a happy gift of nature
    or a strain of madness
                    no
    numb though our limbs grow and few
    though the hours before dawn
    it won't do to listen too
    intently when those cries come
    booming out of the dark
                  so
    the few remaining owls that
    have raged with us before or
    fall gloomy with us after
    are soon still in their first woe
    of sunlight asking nothing

    while morning gives us new roles
    and lifts us who awake whom
    it wakes quite out of ourselves

9 When night falls upon the woods
  and even words like *snout* or
  writhe take on a strange kind of
  loveliness and power
                              look
  how the moon scrabbles over
  the clouds with the simpleness
  of a clown who has never found
  what he sings of in what
  he loves
              the perishable
  rubble of flesh the lustful
  water of eyes muggy warmth
  sweet in the wrinkling skin seems
  all there is and enough too
  Joy commands the natural
  obscene places in dim light
  and pain is only music
  song of long satisfied grunts
  and snapping twigs
                          when a boy
  and a girl like you and me
  humping under the trees in
  musk and wet of our bodies
  fall apart and remember
  gladness in the tongue of larks
  and grief in the knife of flesh
  you can tell morning has come
  with his washbowl and his piece
  of soap and his long prayers

10 Make us stronger, fill our skulls
    with the hollow balls of grief
    Undo the light let the leaves
    plunge unheard, rouse the ghosts of
    beasts, push our face to the ground
    reach into our bowels, scoop
    our pity out and cut girls
    loose from their tangled roots
                                    Night
    restore love, give us loss back

    We lie sweating under bulbs
    bite hard on the pennies
    in our dry mouths and we twist
    rings on our fingers. We write
    the litanies of sexes
    across walls of chalk. We force
    the tight lips of brides apart
    and pry the teeth of brothers
    open. We curl up and hide
    our hands between our thighs
                                    Night
    spend us. We are your money
    We are your vessels, break us

    before the morning revives
    bad seed in the stale water

44

11 The furnace cold, a silver
    moth unmoving in the moss
    of soot up the smoke-stack
    Look up! and the wind and the
    darkness flow across a hole
    not bright enough to nudge you
    into flight
                The moon fumbles
    through the dead hair of the night
    a beetle on the mother's
    body, gropes through the fir trees
    laced round the rim of the earth
    through her hem of ashes clouds
    or dust in the lap of space

    When the pale white scarab halts
    to fill up the chimney mouth
    ringed in his halo of tar t
    he hard eye of the moth glints
    uncertain ruby the furred
    tentative foot of the moth shifts
    Up! and your stunned flight now
    a droplet of quicksilver
    dashed into a bowl of milk

    your small life all cheerfully
    dashed soon into the morning

12 The blunt staves of the darkness
    have been reverently raised
    Thrusting the tribes advance
    Mitered heads block out all light
    White spiders hover in black vaults
    The tribes retreat The walls
    shiver imperceptibly
    The spiders shift position
    Webs have rearranged themselves

    Kings move scepters up and down
    Lovers clasp and unclasp Breath
    comes goes while children
    are photographed in wombs Some
    die more quickly some more slow-
    ly
        Morning shows how it's all
    an exercise of fancy

13 Aubade

When at night a brightness comes
and our two-backed ghost appears
writhing in the forbidden
place behind the glass make me
easy tell me this is not
the last night in the last night
all the rooms of our bodies
are entered and no mirrors
can make obstruction
                    When I
strain to see your face in your
shadow shape but only feel
my own eyes roll in my skull
make me a sign and tell me
this is not the last night in
the last night the dark behind
our eyes marries with the dark
we look out on
                    When something
about the chill of our room makes
me in my skeleton
shiver reach to touch you while
all the trumpets in the blood
breathe *Now the dawn comes! the dawn comes
now!* tell me it is not now
in the last night out souls
hang discarded in their frames
silent air in flutes of bone

and there can be no morning

SERENADES

1 We two are contained by nothing not even this palpable darkness
   Where horns are forgiving us flutes are like bones expectantly still
   And violins are presenting vast night to us in a tiny casket
   We press It between us when we embrace we feel it when we kiss
   Each other's eyes and are not ungrateful for our little present
   Galaxies rustle faintly multitudinous in it and over
   The small blue pearl of its earth animal presences echo
   Their infinitesimal crotchets of yearning through hollow dark
   The violins making a gift of it to us in a tiny casket
   There the hairy hands of the violators the heels of the clumsy
   Suffer ecstatic reduction becoming transparent and frail

   There cruel man stares at his sky with a rush of elegiac feeling
   And dreams of terrific disclosures indefinitely withheld
   Flutes expectantly still like his bones the horns forgiving him:
   Never again will we waken to silence never again
   Hear other than this fading impartial inward singing
   "I am a palpable darkness: You two are contained by nothing."

2 Muted measures lift slab after slab from hollowly gorgeous
   Night *trala* their single refrain discards the romance
   Of epitaphs our great tablets of law are tumbled aside
   With sober inquisitive canons *trarira trala* the bricks
   Of our comfort already crumble near a trampled dancing-floor
   And music's cool contemptuous wisdom whistling digs *trala*
   In the disenchanting ground *trala* casting up our cheap
   Plaster bas-reliefs of *trala* an idyll of mercy
   An allegory of sublime chastisement with easy instruments
   Our mysterious obelisks are felled our pyramids are
   Unpiled *trala* Where are our *'je-ne-sais-quois'* *trala*
   our sweet ineffable *tra* our *la* intimations of *li* . . .
   A pitiless unison turns the last stone to find beneath it
   Ourselves blind white worms left suddenly in morning silence
   Our spontaneity destroyed by our knowledge of what is required

3 Night stretches all her wires tight to lure the sightless
   Heirs of wretchedness here or there or another place
   Strings of silver or steel singing pass from stars
   To tipped grasses tie frost to tree-bark transfix the apples
   With worms or steadily pull at the ring in the nostrils of
   A patient white bull the moon: night organizes courts
   Of desire where all things squirm or thrill at appointed centers
   The bat secure at the place of the moth the moth rejoicing
   In a mansion of little flames the flame ringing a last faint
   Vibration of venom and honeycomb:
                                        Night has tuned her wires
   Precisely has strung them through the ears of her blinded
   Inheritors is making them yearning for justice try to guess
   At the one the final direction by piercing melodies crossing
   Recrossing turning their heads this way or that: they know
   Their eyes no longer avail in the magical night they listen
   For the seat of the harpist themselves musical with regret
   That it beckons from no place that two ears are not enough

4 There while in unromantic branches assembled the air
Unobeyed now sings the counsels of her end he leads her out
Reluctant to hear the refusal of leaves again she allows
His tugging her toward his own significance in the darkness
In May-time one voice can be taken for another she smiles
Brave at his easy merging with the chorus of general talk

"Ah!" he is waving his arms and "Ah!" she has caught his drift
For him the abandon of storm is meaning but she understands
How wisdom is wind except for a trembling in what hangs on
In the leaves that cry: "Don't let him think on autumn nor the moon
Come out to illumine what shivers gray under judgment here
Don't let him remember why winter winds more silently move

Let us all sing to fill him with the grief he will need one day
When he sees the breeze read destruction in a flutter of her blouse."

5　"Ladies and gentlemen," overwrought cries the moon, "I want
　　I want . . . " but he can't conclude he makes a Byronic gesture
　　Pacing spoiled boy his palace with antediluvian frown
　　Among the moist-eyed lovers abstracted murmurs rise
　　The midnight having tried too hard for tone resigns
　　Stars sit in dismayed committees and stare their minutes over
　　While ardor already seizes the reins with easy inaptitude
　　By two o'clock the winds are thick with unassimilated
　　Sighs the commerce of kissing taking an unhealthy turn
　　The traffic of hands in dalliance almost routinely theatrical

　　Ladies and gentlemen take good stock of your naked bodies
　　Do not allow too much currency to protestation for now
　　The darkness is no longer governed in your private interest
　　Your whole wealth a dumb figure asleep in your arms
　　And by four the dew will begin to pluck its weak guitar
　　The cheap sparrows to advertise a narrow sunrise

6 In the plenitude of twelve o'clock the strawberry blood surmises
   Ecstasies of spilling and galaxies are whelming the blackness
   In transcendental frauds the consolations of metaphysical
   Malice outspeed the nimblest afflatus of vulgar happiness
   And gaiety rides her dogcart into the pulsing quasars
   Before formulations of clemency opened the curtains of tears
   Night has stood in the pit darting a lovely scorn and long after
   The echoes of yearning cease in the source a great sanity
   Will gently open her violent book and read a single
   Uncoded word: ENOUGH!
                          O midnight your mothers offer
   Their virtues to the stars and spill their milk in your storms
   Your myriad nebulae transform their infanticides into hymns
   And the black iridescence of plague adorns your maidenly pallors
   Only I your bastard beg for morning on earth for a cold light
   An insomniac staring with electrical aspect into his mirror
   To find there the face of art in all its potential stupidity

7   Now leeks are greening under starlight and glacial ridges flow
    To fill a gentian stratosphere with elfin ghosts of water
    My littleness is wheeling above an alpine dream of your face:
    Sideways from corners of your shrewd closed eyes the wrinkles
    Weave slow laces of lady-wisdom your parted mouth breathes
    Like a chasm from innocent moist lungs rhythmic to smash and lunge
    Of frangible pulses it is Sunday in your spine though the moon's
    Diplomacy still matters in your blood while shambling he wanes
    Feeble in ultramarine profundities of shattered stars:
    If gnats flew alone mountain-high exalted in the salt night
    If they saw your pastoral shape so enormously disposed on a slope
    As I do and understood how ice melting and pungencies of pale green
    Assimilate your hair and your harmonious futures and if
    They outlived the chill to settle at your side in morrowing sun
    Sniffing the fragrances of your unbecoming dream their chorus
    Would retrieve from the tides of the night something I never will
    Who can only remember what I have been told: *She is asleep*

8 Radiance of your body will reach my eyes again but now you lie
   Naked in pitch black as though your frailty had outlawed pity
   Above these clouds the stars in their pride of completed lives
   Probably strut the eternal kids in their quotidian fashion
   Making game of the hearts they steal to their gravity making marriages
   Of all to all in their consummate abodes thank heaven a blanket
   Of unspent rain can hide their stark regard and hallow
   The thrill of darkness torn from startled shadow in the dark
   And it is you love you alone whom now I turn to
   Alone to bring home to you stern axioms of perished stars
   For all nocturnal feelings are versions of panic: still
   I want to speak dimply to you but is it simple to cry
   I love your life which is half done your endurance in divorces
   Your having borne issue who also will cease and your terror
   Of the heart steeling itself for the end of your delight my delight?

9 All day wasted shifting ground to appease you with pledges
Now the air is posting a chilling message to my newest address:
'Nothing is enough take leave of your senses promise her nothing'
Again the beacons of departure have begun to solicit the evening
And the horizon's old cincture yields to their older astral fret
Empty as boats that strain at their moorings the images of desire
Tear against their origins and drift abandoned in cold: You
Whose loving once harnessed my love are hard to find in that dark
Where syllable by syllable my oaths return to encumber me—confessions
Declarations cloy my passage and the words the worlds of my vows
Are all too much: Only your ultimate future flagged
With your name flares austerely from beyond the Milky Way
All other names of desire are beguiling lies I will promise
Nothing: Here is the hand of an idiot on your mortal skin
Here my unpledging mouth looks to yours for the gift of silence
These my five senses are lost in your pitiless fugitive sense
Only your present body saves mine from being inconsolable
Later I fall benighted into nothing between your legs
And nothing is enough as fall together senseless into sleep
Should dawn remember to restore our girding firmament I
Calling back my former senses will fumble to unhasp the chain
Of desire and find no more than a leash of lovely longing

10 ANOTHER YEAR

Snow and the violet see each other satisfied: you will pass
Foolish seeds open wet hands now you see it now you don't
It hammers in the porches a dawning disappointment but but

But it is warm is definite to a fault and it doesn't matter
And you can't render it back not in the heat of this not yet
Nor when King Woodpecker remembers his vengeance when forest was

Was more than this fall of ghosts huddled in metallic regiments
Scratching tomorrow upon the chill stones of their eighth day
Nor yet while brown moss and rain cloud the spring. Keep it then!

A golden eye for your Christmas tree pretending it belongs there
Until the grandsons your enemies crowd secretly back into buds
Green leaves recollected in passing sentences: returned

ELEGY

(In Memory of Hannah Arendt)

Praying the leaves not to sprout, the worlds nevermore to fashion
Coincidences he can homestead for whatsoever
He plans to deserve, he boards his ship and speeds away in
A line impossibly straight tracing the graph of all points
Farthest from complicity
                        You, lady, who have quarreled
(Or with whom he has) are appalled now to rediscover
His tale of your ugliness in the bald twigs of the last
Tree on earth under which you sleep and from which no apple
To bless your kin or curse it will fall until his return.

Nothing is perfect and by your flaws we remember you
And tell you from the perfect others that cannot exist
Yet even so we refuse to recognize what we have
A share in, to be at home with you where all disappoints
But love which is not enough
                        We are the majority
The nations that embarrass you by staring at the scars
On your belly not suiting our manifest destinies
Though you are ours and agree with us when we acclaim
The voyager whose goal shrouds your form in criteria

As for myself can I ever be free of these others
With their insistent statistic that your breasts are too small
Even if lovely, their conceit of your years and seasons
As congenital obstacles to their strait and narrow
Idea, their fear of periphery
                        Let me whisper
To your sleep, change your nightmare of your own grotesqueness
Of your chastity fouled by him who cannot dwell in it
Whom crowds exalt: it is he who abandons you not I
I am another doomed to depart another time

61

I say to them: She dreams and with every cry at her ear
Of *Not enough!* or of *How long? how long?* she is returned
Closer to her ancient but no longer innocent shape
But each time more removed from the embrace of who alone
Can make her know herself lovely
                                   But with them I must cry
At your ear: You are ungenerous you respect neither
Yourself nor our craving for the empire of perfection
You are too obedient to us yet you will not forgive
Miscalculations . . . You environ us with blemishes

I have no desire either to explain or accuse
After all interpretation after discomforting
Intimations of shared petulance time overtakes me
With a rage for utopias, even utopias
That accede to your degradation
                                   There the unlikely
Cocksure lover nursing his knowledge of the perfect face
Smiles on yours despite what failings he has marked on it
I can be dazzled by seas of desolation when I
Enjoy the vantage point of the moon of my perfection

The voyager craves a novelty that will no longer
Surprise him flees from the irritations of your household
Where each hour a new strangeness stuns and renders him guilty
Flees your smiling gravity toward an inner straitness
And after him the multitudes yearn
                                   He has forsaken
Whom before he instructed to feel a necessity
For him alone and he does not remember whether he
Has quarreled or been quarreled with by your ravaged frailty
He can no longer distinguish a strangeness from a flaw

Lady, call him back from accident to coincidence
And forgive us for inventing him, show us all the path
To a knowledge not of faults but of our complicity
And forgive me for what I become among these others
Then free yourself
                    You still speak as one who belongs to me
Your damaged recurrence is not yet irretrievably
Altered so long as you but sleep and a single tree stands
I alone while yet your breath comes am your bridegroom who learns
To let human enterprise cease before your beauty dies

Max Wickert was born in Augsburg, Germany, and immigrated to the United States at age fourteen. Educated at Saint Bonaventure University and Yale University, he taught English in the University at Buffalo from 1966 until his retirement in 2006. He has published two other collections of verse, *Pat Sonnets* (2000) and *No Cartoons* (2011), as well as numerous poems in journals. His short story, "The Scythe of Saturn" was among the winners of the first *Stand Magazine* International Fiction Competition (Newark-on-Tyne, England). He has also published verse translations of two works by Torquato Tasso: *The Liberation of Jerusalem* (Oxford University Press, 2009) and *Love Poems for Lucrezia Bendidio* (Italica Press, 2011). His co-translation into German (with Hubert Kulterer) of Tuli Kupferberg's *1001 Ways to Live Without Working*, originally published in Austria (1972), was recently reissued in Germany. Max Wickert has been Director of the Outriders Poetry Project since its inception.